Pretty Paisleys

Adult Coloring Book

© 2015 Creative Soul Publishing Inc.

Bonus Pages

To receive more downloadable coloring pages visit

www.coloringbookcorner.com

www.ingramcontent.com/pod-product-compliance
Lightning Source LLC
Chambersburg PA
CBHW081150040426

42445CB00015B/1825